*MUSIC THROUGHOUT HISTORY*™

# BEETHOVEN'S WORLD

JENNIFER VIEGAS

rosen publishing's
# rosen central®

New York

*To Lori Cuthbert, Paul Soul Johnson, Martha Rix,*
*and other musicians who, like Beethoven, reveal truth,*
*beauty, and the power within through their music*

Published in 2008 by The Rosen Publishing Group, Inc.
29 East 21st Street, New York, NY 10010

First Edition

**Library of Congress Cataloging-in-Publication Data**

Viegas, Jennifer.
Beethoven's world / Jennifer Viegas.
    p. cm.—(Music throughout history)
ISBN-13: 978-1-4042-0724-0
ISBN-10: 1-4042-0724-4 (library binding)
1. Beethoven, Ludwig van, 1770–1827. 2. Composers—
Austria—Biography. I. Title. II. Series.
ML410.B4V72 2008
780.92—dc22
[B]

2005028917

*Manufactured in the United States of America*

**On the cover:** Portrait of Beethoven composing his *Missa
solemnis*, by Joseph Karl Stieler (1781–1858).

# CONTENTS

In this artist's rendering, the great composer is shown deep in thought, with quill pen in hand. Beethoven sometimes struggled for years before he felt a symphony was complete.

# INTRODUCTION

Ludwig van Beethoven is a rare example of someone who was of his time, and yet, in many ways, ahead of his time. His life played out like one of his beautiful symphonies, with unimaginable highs, lows, victories, and defeats. He devoted much of his life to his music, which inspires listeners even today. Through it, he changed history and influenced the way people view themselves and the world in which they live.

When Beethoven was born in 1770, extremely wealthy monarchs and their appointed regional leaders ruled most of Europe. Privileged aristocrats shared in the wealth and the power, while most others struggled to feed their families. It was nearly impossible to break through such a tight social order. Even the most talented and popular musicians of the day had a hard time improving their status. Franz Joseph Haydn, for example, is now considered one of history's greatest classical composers. But during his lifetime, he essentially was in a social class with liveried, or high-ranking, servants.

Class distinctions still exist today, but they were more evident three centuries ago. At the French royal palace at Versailles, for example, more than 100 people helped the kings and their queens to dress. Royalty got together at least three times a week, enjoying parties that featured mountains of food, wine, gambling, dancing, and music performed by the most popular stars of the day. It was a world closed to all but a privileged few.

By 1827, the year of Beethoven's death, most of these things had changed. Beethoven had been born into the Holy Roman Empire. This was a political ordering of lands that included today's Germany, the Czech Republic, Austria, Liechtenstein, Slovenia, Belgium, and Luxembourg. During various periods, the empire also encompassed parts of Switzerland, Italy, France, Poland, and the Netherlands. In 1827, the Holy Roman Empire was history. The old political order did not exist.

A growing middle class assumed much of the dominance previously held by the aristocracy. This newly empowered class was called the *bourgeoisie*, a French word that refers to traders, merchants, and other working-class people who represent the class between the serfs, or peasants, and the nobility. The change did not come without bloodshed. Louis XIV, a French king who had once enjoyed all of the riches of Versailles, was executed, along with his family, as part of the public's desire to topple the old regime.

During this period of violent, revolutionary change, music reflected the feelings of the times. Some pieces provided a soothing reminder of old traditions that people wanted to keep. Other pieces brought musicians together in powerful harmony, representing the unified bourgeoisie and inspiring them to go forward with their social and economic revolution. At the center of this musical grandeur was Beethoven. Like a composer for an epic movie, he helped to define real-life events as he was contributing to them.

He also redefined the image of composers in society. Before him, even famous composers such as Wolfgang Amadeus Mozart had difficulty breaking through the old aristocratic social order. Mozart, in fact, died close to penniless, and his body was placed in an unmarked grave during a funeral ceremony that was attended by only a handful of mourners. Mostly through the sheer force of his own character, Beethoven rose to greater heights within European society. He was a person with enormous creative talent, and he knew it.

In his biography of Beethoven, Stephen Johnson writes about a letter Beethoven sent to a Viennese royal named Prince Karl Lichnowsky. In the late 1700s, the prince was a patron who provided money, room, and board to Beethoven so that Beethoven might continue to compose music. In the letter, he wrote, "Prince, what you are, you are by accident of birth; what I am, I am of myself. There are and there will be thousands of princes. There is only one Beethoven."

In writing that letter, Beethoven expressed what countless middle-class people felt. Here, at last, was a visionary who earned his success through talent and hard work. For anyone who has ever felt discouraged by social, financial, or personal difficulties, Beethoven's life and music serve as a reminder that greatness is attainable by all of us. With determination, talent, and hard work, an individual's inner voice can touch the lives of countless others and may even transcend the limits of a lifetime.

# CHAPTER ONE

## Beethoven's Childhood

**W**e don't know exactly when Ludwig van Beethoven was born, but he was baptized on December 17, 1770, in the scenic town of Bonn. Bonn is now in western Germany, but in the eighteenth century, Germany did not exist. Instead, the area was part of the Holy Roman Empire, which was formed in AD 800, with the goal of uniting church and state leadership. Although the empire existed for approximately 1,000 years, its vastness made it difficult to manage. For example, the German-speaking population in the Holy Roman Empire lived in 300 separate states. Unlike states today, each of these areas had its own army, leaders, and currency. Since average citizens did not travel as much as people do today, sometimes individuals would never know what life was like outside of their own tiny corner of the empire.

Many of Germany's states were ruled by electors— men who had the privilege of electing the Holy Roman Emperor. Bonn was in the Electorate of Cologne and served as its capital. The city also had a palace that was presided over by the archbishop elector of Cologne. At the time of Beethoven's birth, this man was Maximilian Friedrich. Typical of most aristocrats of his day, Friedrich, by most accounts, cared little about the concerns of the poor but a lot about art, architecture, and music. This being the case, a person who was not a royal and did not hold some other important title would do well by going into one of these three creative trades. Beethoven's grandfather made this wise decision.

## LUDWIG VAN BEETHOVEN, THE ELDER

Beethoven's grandfather, whom the composer was named after, died when Beethoven was only three years old, but young Beethoven idolized him nonetheless. The elder Beethoven studied in the choir school of St. Rombaut before he was appointed choir director of the church of St. Pierre in Louvain, Belgium. Later, he began singing and playing the organ at another church, the St. Lambert Cathedral. There he gained public recognition for his deep bass voice and musical talents.

He then moved to Bonn, where he was given an appointment that put him in charge of music performed at Bonn's chapel, concert hall, theater, and court ballroom. If an event involved music in Bonn, chances were Beethoven's grandfather was involved in the project.

Since he held a prominent position, the elder Beethoven received a good, steady salary, which he supplemented with earnings from a wine business.

His private life was less successful and foreshadowed some of the tensions and problems that his famous grandson would later face. In 1733, Beethoven's grandfather married Maria Josepha Poll. She was supposedly an alcoholic and, because of this, the family placed her in a cloister, which is a restricted area within a monastery or convent. Women in these times often were "put away" in such places if they did not get along with their husbands, suffered from psychological problems or drug abuse, or were otherwise unwanted by their families. Sometimes the husband or others received money because they gained control of the cloistered woman's inheritance. Beethoven never visited his grandmother and never spoke about her. His grandparents had three children, but only one of them survived into adulthood. The child was Johann van Beethoven, the composer's father.

## PARENTS: JOHANN VAN BEETHOVEN AND MARIA MAGDALENA KEVERICH

Although no official record of his birth exists, Johann van Beethoven was born in either 1739 or 1740. Like his father, he possessed a gift for music, but not to the same degree. He was a tenor singer and became a teacher of piano, violin, and voice. In 1767, Johann married Maria Magdalena Keverich, in Bonn.

Maria, the daughter of a cook, was not fully accepted by Johann's father. He felt that she was beneath the station of his son and the Beethoven family. Johann, perhaps

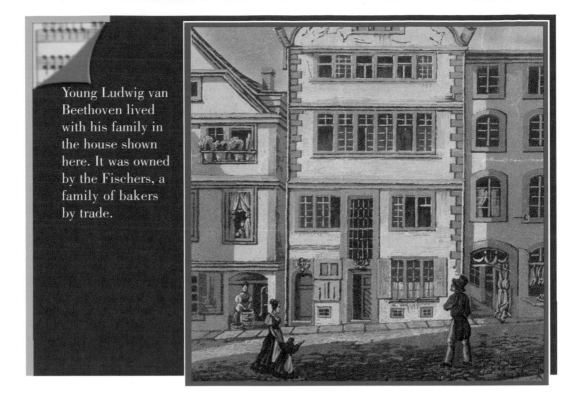

Young Ludwig van Beethoven lived with his family in the house shown here. It was owned by the Fischers, a family of bakers by trade.

tired of being bullied by his father, defied his father's wishes and married her. Maria had already been married once before, to a young man who died two years after they wed, leaving her a widow before she turned eighteen years old. She was twenty-one when she married Johann.

In his Beethoven biography, Maynard Solomon tells about accounts written by members of the Fischer family, who owned and lived in a home with the Beethovens. According to the Fischers, Johann and Maria did not enjoy a very happy marriage. In fact, in the late 1700s, Maria was said to have remarked to a young woman, "If you want to take my good advice, remain single, and then you will have the most tranquil, most beautiful, most pleasurable life. For what is marriage? A little joy, but then a chain of sorrows." As time would tell, Maria's son Ludwig may have taken this advice to heart.

Johann and Maria had seven children, but only three of these survived into adulthood. All three were boys: Ludwig, who was the eldest son, Kaspar Anton Karl, and Nikolaus Johann. The family occupied several rooms in the Fischers' comfortable and spacious house. Home life was complicated by the fact that Johann could never equal his father's achievements. As a musician, he was not as well regarded as his father, and according to many accounts, this contributed to his alcoholism.

In 1774, after the death of his father, Johann attempted to fill the position he once held but was rejected. Distraught, Johann began to drink more and to withdraw from his family in the evenings by going to taverns or wandering around town. His greatest hope for success in life now rested on one individual—his young son Ludwig.

## FATHER AND SON

Very little is known about the composer's first years of life. When Ludwig was four or five, his father began to give him music lessons. He taught Ludwig how to play the violin and the clavier, which is a general term for instruments with a keyboard, such as a piano or harpsichord. According to Denise Balcavage's biography, some people who knew him regarded Johann as a very stern and possibly abusive teacher. Cäcilia Fischer—a daughter in the Fischer family, in whose house the Beethovens used to live—remembered young Ludwig as "a tiny boy standing on a little footstool in front of the clavier, to which the implacable severity of his father had so early condemned him." Another account provided by the music historian Francois-Joseph Fétis, a contemporary of

Beethoven's, said that "Beethoven's father used violence when it came to making him [Ludwig] start his musical studies, and . . . there were few days when he was not beaten in order to compel him to set himself at the piano." Yet another account, authored by Court Councillor Kruff, said that Johann "sometimes shut him up in the cellar."

Since these events took place when Beethoven was at such an impressionable age, it is hard to tell how much of his later obsession with music came from love of his craft or from a drive instilled by his domineering father. The two must have merged in his mind because the lessons, however severe, helped to mold a child of extraordinary talent. Much of this talent was natural, as other pushy parents of the past and present have tried to create child prodigies to no avail. In Beethoven's time, the model of youthful success was Mozart.

While Mozart was attractive and outgoing, Beethoven was perpetually unkempt and emotionally withdrawn. Beethoven often had messy hair, did not receive regular baths, and wore old, torn clothing. His music was always most important. Some historians even believe that the young musician created a fantasy life for himself. Naturally dark-skinned, he was given the nickname "der Spagnol," or "the Spaniard," by some observers. Beethoven reveled in this idea, and, later in life, he hesitated in correcting false claims that he could have been the secret child of some Spanish royal. The word "von" indicated someone of noble birth, while "van" meant "from" in Flemish and was just a common part of certain European names, like "Mc" or "Mac" before Scottish surnames. In keeping with his fantasy background, Beethoven did not correct writers who misspelled his last name "von Beethoven."

## Wolfgang Amadeus Mozart

Mozart was born in 1756, nearly two decades before Beethoven. However, the legacy of his childhood brilliance still thrived in the late eighteenth century, even after Mozart died in 1791, at the young age of thirty-five. Beethoven's early life paralleled that of Mozart, who also began musical studies with his father around the age of four. He, too, studied keyboard instruments and showed talent at that age. Mozart had an older sister, Maria Anna, who also possessed enormous talent as a youngster.

When Mozart was just six years old and his sister, Maria, was eleven, their father arranged for them to play concerts for the elector of Bavaria, at Munich, and for the Empress Maria Theresa, in Vienna. The royals loved the young musicians, and word quickly spread to their aristocratic friends that a new talented duo was in their midst. Soon, all of their European friends and family wanted to hear the Mozarts. In 1763, Mozart and his sister played concerts in Paris, France, and London, England, before the monarchs there. When Mozart was seven, he already was composing original music. By 1769, he had authored four pieces for the piano, his first symphonies, and at least one opera, *The Pretend Simpleton*.

Mozart's relationship with his father remains controversial to this day. Some historians claim that his father was a brutal man who beat his young son. Others say the family enjoyed a close and loving relationship. One fact is clear: Mozart enjoyed enormous success as a child, and many other parents, particularly those in the music field, wanted their children to equal or surpass Mozart's legacy.

## FIRST CONCERT

Beethoven, like Mozart, showed a gift for composition early on. Even so, Beethoven's father is said to have at first discouraged his son from playing his own music in favor of more rigorous study. In 1778, Beethoven's father agreed that Ludwig was ready to be showcased, so he arranged for a concert in Cologne, a city not far from Bonn. Unlike Mozart, Beethoven was not an immediate smash hit. But his father's colleagues and other local musicians did begin to take notice of him.

## SCHOOL

Few historical records exist concerning Beethoven's other education, but he probably attended a Bonn elementary school from ages six to eleven. Regular courses of instruction then were reading, writing, math, religion, Latin, and choir. He excelled at foreign languages, which would help him later, when he traveled and composed music for diverse audiences.

Mathematics and writing vexed him. He was a poor writer who always had trouble spelling and communicating his thoughts and feelings on paper. According to Balcavage, Beethoven once wrote to his friend Franz Wegeler, "I often compose the answer in my mind, but when I wish to write it down, I usually throw the pen away because I cannot write as I feel."

As writing was difficult, Beethoven found solace in his music. At the keyboard or through his violin, he could express himself freely. Based on his own remarks, his music became the audible manifestation of his innermost feelings. Considering that he was about to produce some of the world's most beautiful and memorable music, he must have held some very powerful thoughts and emotions within himself.

# CHAPTER TWO
## Mentors and Friends

**D**espite the harsh teaching methods used by his father, Beethoven absorbed the instructions. There also are indications that the household was not always a place of misery. Biographer Maynard Solomon relates an account provided by Cäcilia Fischer that indicates that at least one day was full of joy and music. Regarding a birthday of Maria Magdalena, Fischer wrote, "Each year, the feast of St. Mary Magdalene (her birthday and name day) was kept with due solemnity. The music stands were brought (in) and placed in the two sitting rooms overlooking the street, and a canopy, embellished with flowers, leaves, and laurel, was put up in the room containing Grandfather Ludwig's portrait. On the eve of the day, Madame van

Beethoven was induced to retire betimes. By ten o'clock all was in readiness. The silence was broken by the tuning up of instruments; Madame van Beethoven was awakened (and) requested to dress, and was then led to a beautifully draped chair beneath the canopy. An outburst of music roused the neighbors, the most drowsy soon catching the infectious gaiety. When the music was over the table was spread and, after food and drink, the merry company fell to dancing (but in stockinged feet to lessen the noise), and so the festivities came to an end."

This episode reveals that the young Beethoven must have experienced at least some fun and love at home. The image of his torturous piano lessons mixed with an all-night celebration is quite a contrast. Perhaps it helps to explain the extreme emotional highs and lows that the composer later felt and put into his music.

## CHRISTIAN GOTTLOB NEEFE

In 1779, a talented German composer, organist, and conductor moved to Bonn. His name was Christian Gottlob Neefe. Well-known in music circles for being a talented and smart individual, Neefe joined Bonn's Grossman and Helmuth theatrical company. He then was given the position of court organist in Bonn, in 1781. Around that time, sensing that his own talents were now far behind those of his son, Beethoven's father hired Neefe to take charge of Beethoven's musical education. That decision was probably the best one he could have made.

Beethoven developed a close relationship with Neefe. Unlike Beethoven's father, Neefe was very cultivated, disciplined, well-read, and interested in new developments concerning history and philosophy. These were subjects that also interested young Beethoven. In addition, Neefe was a great admirer of Johann Sebastian Bach. Some people felt that Bach's music was antiquated, or out of date, but Neefe and Beethoven knew better.

About 1721, Bach compiled two Clavierbüchlein (little keyboard books) for his wife. These contained beautiful and complex musical works for both large and small groups of musicians. He also wrote a keyboard collection called *The Well-Tempered Clavier*. Today we take it for granted that we can buy sheet music or download it off the Internet. In Beethoven's time, however, much of the music was available only in painstakingly copied handwritten versions, such as the Bach pieces Neefe presented to Beethoven. The young student approached the assignment with earnest. Neefe immediately recognized Beethoven's talent, and, in 1782, Neefe trained his student to be his assistant as a court organist. That same year, he arranged for Beethoven to become an orchestra director, a position in which the young pianist would conduct while playing the piano. This skill would serve him well later.

Inspired by his new mentor, Beethoven began approaching his own musical compositions more seriously. He had always enjoyed making up tunes, but now he realized that, like Bach, he, too, might one day become a great composer. Neefe and Beethoven's parents probably filled his mind with such dreams.

## EARLY COMPOSITIONS

Beethoven's earliest surviving composition is a set of keyboard variations on a march written by Ernst Christoph

When he was only twelve years old, Beethoven played this organ during morning mass at the Minorite Church St. Remigius, in Bonn.

Dressler. Neefe saw the quality in his student's work and, around 1782, decided to publish Beethoven's compositions. One of the most interesting aspects of the variations was that Beethoven composed the piece in the key of C minor. That means the notes in the composition correspond to a certain tonal chord (the key). In the case of C minor, the mood of the key gives the music a very dark sound. So, through his variations, young Beethoven displayed his mastery at composing and, at the same time, challenged himself and other musicians who attempted to play his complicated works.

Musicologists, or people who study music as a branch of knowledge, refer to this time in Beethoven's life as his First Period. It includes all of his early compositions, which began to pour out while he was still a student of Neefe's. In his biography of Beethoven, Barry Cooper mentions that

Neefe, trying to publicize the talent of his pupil, had a notice printed in a popular music magazine. Published on March 2, 1783, the announcement read: "Louis van Beethoven [note that his first name was misprinted] . . . a boy of eleven years and of most promising talent. He plays the clavier very skillfully and with power, reads at sight very well, and—to put it in a nutshell—he plays chiefly The Well-Tempered Clavier of Sebastian Bach, which Herr Neefe put into his hands . . . This youthful genius is deserving of help to enable him to travel. He would surely become a second Wolfgang Amadeus Mozart were he to continue as he has begun."

Note that Beethoven's age is listed as eleven, when he was actually twelve. Some historians theorize that Beethoven's father intentionally deceived others, and perhaps even Beethoven himself, about the boy's age. It is likely that he hoped it would create a reputation for Beethoven as a child prodigy, like Mozart.

Just as Beethoven had outgrown the teachings of his father, now he was ready to seek other education outside of Bonn and beyond Neefe. As the magazine announcement indicated, though, he needed funds to do all of this. No one immediately came to his financial rescue, so Beethoven became a tutor to the children of Stephan von Breuning, a wealthy Bonn resident. Breuning adored Beethoven, who often spent a lot of time in his home. Franz Wegeler, a friend and confidant of Beethoven's, said that at the von Breuning home, Beethoven "was treated as one of the children of the family, and he spent not only the greatest part of the day there, but even many nights" (as quoted in Stephen Johnson's *Ludwig van Beethoven: An Essential Guide to His Life and Works*).

## THE ENLIGHTENMENT

The late eighteenth century was a period in history when scholars emphasized reason as the best way for determining the truth about life. This philosophy was developed during the Enlightenment period, which began in the 1600s and lasted through the 1700s. Before the Enlightenment, monarchs viewed themselves as appointed by God, believing they had supreme authority over their subjects. However, when people began to learn more about science, politics, law, and education, they started to realize that each person possessed a mind of his or her own. This meant that individuals had a rational will, or the ability to think for themselves and to control their own lives. God no longer chose European monarchs; rational humans did.

Enlightenment thinking brought about revolutionary scientific advancements, typified by the work of British scientist Sir Isaac Newton (1642–1727), who described the laws of gravity and motion. This new philosophy about life radically changed the way most people viewed their place in the world.

## MAXIMILIAN FRANZ

In 1784, Maximilian Franz became the new elector of the region in which Beethoven lived. Franz was the brother of Queen Marie Antoinette of France, the son of the Holy Roman Emperor Francis I, and the brother of the Austrian ruler Emperor Joseph II. With so many royal family connections, Franz carried enormous influence and power throughout Europe. He also had one driving passion: music.

A man of his times, Franz was firmly part of the ruling class. But as a product of Enlightenment thinking, he was open to new ideas and talent, even from people who were not born into his class. Franz maintained a court orchestra in which Beethoven played the viola. As a string player, Beethoven made a name for himself because he played more complicated pieces, like some of Mozart's operas, with ease. In time, word reached Franz that his viola player also had phenomenal keyboard and composing skills. As a result, in 1787, Franz sponsored Beethoven's long-awaited trip to Vienna, Austria.

At this time, Vienna was a vibrant cultural center of Europe that attracted many musicians. It is likely that Franz made his decision to sponsor Beethoven after being urged by Count Ferdinand Ernst Gabriel von Waldstein, the youngest son of one of the Holy Roman Empire's most influential and wealthy families. Von Waldstein admired Beethoven and promoted the young composer's works whenever possible, speaking favorably about him with his powerful friends, including Franz.

## First Trip to Vienna

Beethoven left Bonn in March 1787. The main purpose of the trip must have been for him to meet Europe's reigning music star, Mozart. Although no official records exist for this happening, many anecdotes suggest that the two composers did indeed meet. Beethoven probably played for Mozart in a crowded room full of listeners eager to discover the next prodigy. Biographer Stephen Johnson wrote that Mozart was said to have commented, "Very pretty, but studied." However, after spending more time with Beethoven, Mozart supposedly concluded, "Keep an eye on him. One day he will give the world something to talk about."

## DEATH OF MOTHER

Only two weeks into the Vienna trip, Beethoven received word that his mother was deathly ill with consumption, or tuberculosis. Maria Magdalena died shortly after Beethoven returned to Bonn. The death devastated Beethoven's father, who tried to ease his depression with alcohol and drugs. In his state, he could no longer handle his position as head of the household, so Beethoven was forced to take charge of the care and welfare of his two younger brothers.

In 1792, five years after the death of Beethoven's mother, Beethoven's father died. This sad news was soon followed by a shocking revelation. Beethoven learned that not only was his father in debt, but he also had spent the money meant for his younger brothers. Beethoven was horrified. By this time, however, he already was earning a good income on his own. His brothers were working as well. Kaspar Carl was a musician who sometimes assisted Beethoven, and Nikolaus Johann became a successful pharmacist who later owned his own shop. With his parents gone and his virtuoso skills still largely untested, it was time for young Beethoven to leave Bonn behind.

# CHAPTER THREE

## Stardom

In 1792, Beethoven again left Bonn for Vienna. Again, Count Ferdinand Ernst Gabriel von Waldstein helped to fund the trip. Von Waldstein was Beethoven's first major patron in Bonn. The system of patronage involves one person or group providing money, or other forms of support and influence, to another individual or group. Usually both sides benefit. In the case of von Waldstein and Beethoven, the count gained social prestige by having such a talented musician under his wing and at his disposal. In fact, von Waldstein is remembered mostly for his patronage of Beethoven. (The composer dedicated his Waldstein Sonata, opus 53, to the count.) Beethoven, in turn, gained financial and social freedoms that otherwise would not have been available to him. The patron gave Beethoven

Vienna, Austria (above), was perhaps the most sophisticated European capital during the latter half of the eighteenth century, when this painting was made.

entry into the aristocratic world, and the young composer gladly accepted the invitation.

Shortly before departing for Vienna, Beethoven met the composer Joseph Haydn (1732–1809), who had traveled to Beethoven's hometown as a stopover on the way to London. Haydn had seen a copy of the Beethoven composition, Cantata on the Death of the Emperor Joseph II. The emperor had died in 1790, and because the emperor's family had been so supportive of Beethoven, the composer poured his heart and soul into this piece. Haydn supposedly took one look at the cantata and agreed to take on Beethoven as a pupil in Vienna. With the recent death of Mozart, everyone, including Haydn, was searching for the next big musical star to fill the void left by Mozart and to reenergize Europe's music scene.

In 1792, Beethoven's star was rising. Stephen Johnson tells about how von Waldstein wrote to Beethoven just before the composer left for Vienna: "Dear Beethoven, You are now going to Vienna in fulfillment of a wish that has for so long been thwarted. The genius of Mozart still mourns and weeps for the death of its protégé. It has found a refuge in the inexhaustible Haydn, but no permanent abode. Through him it desires once more to find a union with someone. Through your unceasing diligence, receive the spirit of Mozart from the hands of Haydn."

Beethoven's trip to Vienna was, at times, treacherous. The French Revolution had begun just three years earlier, and now France had declared war on Austria. Fortunately, Beethoven survived the trip and arrived in Vienna on November 10. He then wrote to his old teacher, Neefe, "Thank you for the advice you have so often given me in the development of my God-given art. If I should ever become a great man, you too will have a share in my success."

The most valuable possession that Beethoven brought from Bonn to Vienna was a letter of introduction from von Waldstein to Prince Karl Lichnowsky. Another aristocratic music lover, Lichnowsky took Beethoven into his home and let him stay in a small apartment in his attic. Beethoven disliked the cramped quarters, but he soon gained favor in the prince's company.

## PRIVATE CONCERTS AND MUSICAL CONTESTS

Wealthy individuals often served elaborate dinners and then brought guests to a large room where a celebrated musician would play a private concert for them. (Consider what it must have been like for Prince Lichnowsky to have Beethoven residing in his home. Think of your favorite performer or band, and then imagine if they lived in your home and could play a private set for you whenever you desired!) Similar to Beethoven's patronage arrangement with von Waldstein, this new setup benefited both Beethoven and the prince. Beethoven received room and board, plus the opportunity to mingle with other influential musicians and patrons of the arts. He now had the financial and personal freedom to spend time on his own compositions.

The patronage system helped Beethoven throughout his life. These were times before the invention of the gramophone, an early record player, so artists could not sell their recordings. Patronage, therefore, provided one of the few ways that musicians could make a living.

For his part, every Friday night, Prince Lichnowsky entertained his friends in a salon. The featured entertainment, of course, was Beethoven, who would play the piano, the cello, the violin, the viola, or other instruments he had mastered. Beethoven was brilliant at improvising, or inventing music in the moment, a way of playing that was later popularized in American jazz. When improvising, he could take a basic melody and build other original melodies out of it. As a result, he was not limited to a set series of compositions. His music during these private concerts often deviated into fresh material that always captivated his audiences.

The prince and others arranged for improvising contests. They would pit Beethoven against challengers who would attempt to invent lengthier and more creative compositions. One such competitor, a pianist named Daniel Steibelt (ca. 1764–1823), selected a theme of Beethoven's to improvise upon in an attempt to mock Beethoven. Not to be outdone, Beethoven invented a brilliant, mocking version of one of Steibelt's works, causing the beaten competitor to storm out in a humiliated huff.

## A TEMPERAMENTAL ARTIST

In less than a month, Prince Lichnowsky moved Beethoven to a huge apartment on the ground floor of his residence. Lichnowsky, who was fourteen years older than Beethoven, treated the composer like a son and as a member of his own family. Beethoven, however, was set in his sloppy ways. He hated having to dress up for dinner and for the Friday concerts. On one occasion, Lichnowsky asked Beethoven at the last minute to play for some French soldiers, but Beethoven refused. Previously, the temperamental artist had walked out on guests. He also canceled performances when he felt slighted, or if he believed his audience was not attentive enough. In this instance, Beethoven stormed out of the house and later threw to the floor a plaster bust that Lichnowsky had given him. However, the prince never doubted the young composer's talent and continued to enjoy listening to his music.

## RELATIONSHIPS WITH OTHER ARTISTS

Throughout his career, Beethoven maintained professional relationships with other musicians and artists. He met George Bridgetower (1780–1860), a celebrated English violinist, shortly after the Englishman settled in Vienna, in 1803. They worked together until an argument over a woman ended their friendship. In Vienna, Beethoven also met Domenico Dragonetti (1763–1846), a famous double bass player from Italy. Many music scholars believe that

Two pages from the score of Beethoven's Symphony no. 2 in D Major. Largely inspired by the works of Franz Joseph Haydn, the Second Symphony demonstrates Beethoven's masterful range and skill.

Dragonetti's playing inspired the beautiful double bass parts in Beethoven's Fifth Symphony. In 1812, Beethoven met one of his favorite writers, Johann von Goethe (1749–1832), in the spa town of Teplitz, Bohemia. Beethoven wrote music for several Goethe poems. While their collaboration worked from an artistic standpoint, they had a turbulent relationship that ended when the composer snubbed one of Goethe's royal friends.

## First Symphonies

In 1799, at the age of twenty-eight, Beethoven composed his first symphony, Symphony no. 1 in C Major, opus 21. (While composers often number their own pieces, the numbering of Beethoven's *opuses*, or "works" in Latin, became part of official titles after he died.) A symphony is a lengthy composition intended to be played by a group of musicians. Usually, symphonies are made up of four movements, or sections. The first movement is an allegro, or a piece of music that is played at a relatively fast tempo. The second movement is slower. The third—normally a minuet—brings up the musical pace again, while the fourth movement returns to the allegro tempo of the first movement.

Beethoven's first symphony debuted at the Imperial Court Theater in Vienna. He dedicated it to one of his patrons, Baron van Swieten (1733–1803), who also helped to support Haydn and Mozart. The piece was reminiscent of Haydn and Mozart's earlier works. However, the prominence of wind instruments, an explosive third movement, and the broad range of emotions that the symphony evokes set Beethoven apart from his fellow composers. He had created a unique, complex sound, and audiences loved it.

People begged him to write another symphony, so he followed up the success of his first work with Symphony no. 2 in D Major, op. 36. This piece premiered in 1802. Like his first symphony, it features a special third movement, but one that is even less like the traditional minuet. It is an audacious, lively composition that can properly be called a scherzo. Overall, Symphony no. 2 is an uplifting and joyous work that carries the listener away on a journey created in Beethoven's mind. Music primarily involves our sense of hearing but, for Beethoven, it was an extension of his internal thoughts. In fact, the great composer often could no longer hear his own music. He was becoming increasingly deaf.

# CHAPTER FOUR

# Tragedy and Innovation

**B**eethoven may have suffered from hearing problems throughout most of his adult life, but the symptoms first became evident in 1796, when he was twenty-six years old. At that time, the composer reported experiencing tinnitus, which is an uncomfortable and distracting buzzing or ringing in the ears. For Beethoven, it happened more often than not. He also felt pain in his ears whenever there was a loud sound. Considering that he worked with symphonies and groups of other musicians who often played loudly, he must have felt excruciating pain quite often.

Carl Czerny (1791–1857), a child piano prodigy who later became known for his own compositions, visited the composer in the winter of 1799 to 1780. Czerny wrote that he found Beethoven dressed in shaggy clothing, unshaven, and with cotton stuck in his ears. The cotton seemed to have been dipped in a liquid. The cotton treatment was one of many "cures" that doctors prescribed. To this day, no one is certain what caused Beethoven's deafness. It may have been caused by an illness or a chronic disease. His doctors were even more perplexed. They could only suggest folk remedies, such as taking hot baths or going on long walks, to try to relieve his suffering.

One common treatment was to simply rest in a quiet, natural setting. So, in April 1802, Beethoven took some time off from his work and traveled to Heiligenstadt, a quaint village north of Vienna favored by wealthy individuals as a summer retreat. While there, he wrote a disturbing (and now famous) letter to his two brothers. The letter, which historians call the "Heiligenstadt Testament," probably was not sent. Therefore, it is believed that no one but Beethoven himself read it during his lifetime. It reveals that he had reached a breaking point.

## THE HEILIGENSTADT TESTAMENT

In his biography of the composer, Maynard Solomon reproduced Beethoven's Heiligenstadt letter, the first part of which reads:

> *For my brothers Carl and [Johann] Beethoven. Oh you men who think or say that I am malevolent, stubborn, or misanthropic, how greatly do you wrong me. You do not know the secret cause which makes me seem that way to you. From childhood on, my heart and soul have been full of*

*the tender feeling of goodwill, and I was even inclined to accomplish great things. But, think that for six years now I have been hopelessly afflicted, made worse by senseless physicians, from year to year deceived with hopes of improvement, finally compelled to face the prospect of a lasting malady (whose cure will take years or, perhaps, be impossible). Though born with a fiery, active temperament, even susceptible to the diversions of society, I was soon compelled to isolate myself, to live life alone. If at times I tried to forget all this, oh how harshly was I flung back by the doubly sad experience of my bad hearing. Yet it was impossible for me to say to people, "Speak louder, shout, for I am deaf." . . . what a humiliation for me when someone standing next to me heard a flute in the distance and I heard nothing, or someone standing next to me heard a shepherd singing and again I heard nothing. Such incidents drove me almost to despair; a little more of that and I would have ended my life—it was only my art that held me back."*

The letter ends as though it could have been meant as a suicide note, since Beethoven bids his brothers farewell. The phrase "it was only my art that held me back" indicates that it was music that saved him. Although so many aspects of his life were adversely affected by his hearing loss, he somehow held on to his music. As Beethoven said earlier in his life, music was his God-given talent. He simply refused to disappoint God, himself, and others.

## BEETHOVEN'S SECOND PERIOD

The Heiligenstadt Testament (1802) marked a turning point in Beethoven's life and career. Perhaps the reminder of his own mortality and failings stimulated his competitive nature and his desire to do as much as he could before he died. The period lasting from about 1800 to 1815 is referred to as Beethoven's Second Period. During these years, he wrote what many consider to be some of the world's best music.

Classical music today contrasts with popular music, a category that includes such styles as rock, pop, jazz, soul, and rhythm and blues. But in Beethoven's day, when "classical" was new, it was one of the most popular forms of music. Usually, most popular songs today only contain a handful of melodies. When Beethoven composed a piece, he filled it with multiple melodies. Often he based them on an original motif, or a recurring theme, within a longer piece of music. Because his works contain so many motifs, longer melodies, and variations on these themes, it may require a bit more effort for the uninitiated to appreciate his creations. The rewards, however, are worth it. His mastery of so many instruments, his creativity, and the emotional depth that he gave his music are almost without compare.

## INSTRUMENTAL AND VOCAL MUSIC

Instrumental music, or music without vocals, can be divided into three basic categories: solo music, chamber music, and orchestral music. Beethoven composed works in all three categories. Solo music is played by a single instrument. Commonly it is for a keyboard instrument, such as a piano, but solo music can be for any instrument. Chamber music is music for small groups of musicians. Often these groups are named for the number of musicians, such as a duo, trio, or quartet. Beethoven often participated in chamber music ensembles when he performed in private homes, where smaller rooms would be ill suited to large groups. Orchestral music is written for larger chamber groups and orchestras that today contain eighty or more musicians. (However, most orchestras in Beethoven's day were smaller.)

Beethoven also composed vocal music, which can be divided into four major types: songs, choral music, operas, and oratorios. Songs, in terms of classical music, refer to pieces for one vocalist, usually accompanied by a piano or sometimes a guitar. Choral music is for groups of vocalists who sing in unison and usually are organized by the tones of their voices. Opera—a type of musical play— brings together songs, or solo music, with choral music and instrumentals. In most operas, the dialogue is sung, although Beethoven's only opera, *Fidelio*, has mostly spoken dialogue. Oratorios, like operas, combine solo pieces, chorus work, and instrumentals, but they usually are organized around a general theme instead of being incorporated into a theatrical story.

## SYMPHONIC AND ORCHESTRAL INSTRUMENTS

People who attend classical music concerts or operas today usually expect to see the same basic instruments. Beethoven brought many of these instruments to the concert stage. Instruments are organized into distinct groups. These include woodwinds, brass, string, and percussion.

## Woodwinds

Woodwinds, as the name suggests, refer to instruments that are either made out of wood, or once were, and require the musician to blow through them. One woodwind, the piccolo, is a small, high-pitched flute. Beethoven was one of the first composers to use the piccolo in a symphony, including them in both Symphony no. 5 and Symphony no. 6. Flutes previously existed, but they began to be made with more keys in the 1700s. The extra keys allowed the player to hit additional notes with greater accuracy. The oboe, an instrument with a cylindrical wooden body that is played by blowing into a special mouthpiece called a double reed, also became especially popular during Beethoven's time. Beethoven, Mozart, and other classical composers wrote solo pieces for the oboe. The clarinet, another woodwind instrument, was not used much until the mid-eighteenth century. Mozart was immediately interested in this instrument, which Beethoven also appreciated.

## Brass

Like woodwinds, brass instruments are played by blowing. But, as their name indicates, they are made out of brass or some other metal. Today we are used to seeing valves on trumpets and other horns, but Beethoven wrote his brass parts for horns without valves. Another brass instrument, the trombone, evolved to its more modern form in the 1700s, and Beethoven was one of the first composers to write parts for trombone players, in his Fifth, Sixth, and Ninth Symphonies.

## Strings and Percussion

The stringed instruments, such as violins, violas, and cellos, were popular since the 1500s, but they became common in orchestras only in the seventeenth and eighteenth centuries. Percussion instruments are some of the world's oldest, but orchestral pieces with stronger, more complex rhythm sections did not develop until more modern times. Keyboard instruments, however, went through a number of radical changes in the 1700s.

Pianos were not even made then. They evolved from an instrument called the harpsichord, which was invented in the early 1400s, in Flanders (along the coast of what is now Belgium). The harpsichord actually belongs to the plucked zither family of instruments. Its strings are plucked with devices made with such materials as quill, leather, and metal. Over time, harpsichords merged with new technology so that inside the sound box of this later type of instrument, strings were not plucked. Instead, they were struck by hammers attached to keys. In the late 1700s, pianos continued to undergo changes, but the sound was very different from that of modern pianos.

The keyboard instruments that Beethoven played had a narrower range of pitches, different action, and smaller frames. They continued to grow in size and power during his lifetime, and he was interested in experimenting with the new expressive capabilities. By featuring these revamped instruments in his works, Beethoven helped define what we now consider a standard orchestra or symphony.

Beethoven was an innovator in ways other than just his use of musical instruments. He was also one of the first men of any profession to break through the rigid class structure that defined European society for so many centuries. He embodied what the French revolutionaries and the Enlightenment philosophers had dreamed about. He was living proof that with hard work and determination, a person could become successful of his or her own free will. It is no wonder that his fame rose in America after the American Revolution, as his principles in many ways mirrored American ideals about free will that still exist to this day. Classical musicians and conductors, including Anthony Philip Heinrich, who immigrated to the United States from European countries, helped to popularize Beethoven's music. In 1817, Heinrich was the first to conduct a Beethoven symphony in the states. He conducted either the First or Third Symphony in Kentucky.

## FROM CLASSICISM TO ROMANTICISM

For many reasons, Beethoven put a great deal of himself into his music. Because of his deafness and inability to write or speak well, music became his primary form of communication. So much feeling and thought went into his compositions. His talent and personality also contributed to the powerful emotions his music stirred in listeners. This went against the norm of classical music, which embodied a philosophy called Classicism. Classicism is a philosophy for art—and life in general—that emphasizes order, balance, simplicity, and lack of emotional extremes. Beethoven certainly was not a simple person, and one listen to his music makes it clear that he imbued his compositions with emotional extremes. Beethoven therefore helped to usher in a new philosophical movement that emphasized passion, creativity, expressiveness,

This painting reflects the passion and intensity of Beethoven's style. With his clenched left hand and long, untamed hair, the conductor seems to embody his powerful music.

imagination, individuality, and spontaneity. This movement is called Romanticism.

Romanticism became the dominant style of arts, philosophy, and literature throughout the entire nineteenth century. Beethoven did not consciously become a Romanticist. He was just following his own inner voice, which resonated with others. Much of the poetry, painting, literature, and, of course, music that was produced during the Romantic era was inspired by Beethoven's work. Other famous Romanticists include American Gothic novelist Washington Irving (1783–1859), poet and author Edgar Allan Poe (1809–1849), British poet William Wordsworth (1770–1850), composer Richard Strauss (1864–1949), and Hungarian pianist and composer Franz Liszt (1811–1886), whom legend has it received a kiss from Beethoven because his music was so moving.

# CHAPTER FIVE
## Second Period Music

The turn of a century always seems to bring about anticipation for change. Consciously or not, this was the case at the dawn of the nineteenth century. Already the French Revolution had altered views about class structure. Concerts given by the great composers now were accessible to more people, not only the nobility. Churchgoers could hear Beethoven's pieces, as could residents of Vienna who were able to attend one or more of the many concerts Beethoven himself orchestrated. Audiences were hungry for music, and between 1800 and 1815, Beethoven satisfied their needs. The huge, sweeping symphonies he wrote during this period reflect the immensely powerful changes that were sweeping over the European continent and the world in general.

# THE SYMPHONIES

## The Eroica

Early in the new century, in 1805, Beethoven debuted one of his great masterpieces, his Symphony no. 3, op. 55, or the Eroica Symphony. The Eroica Symphony, or Heroic Symphony, was written for Napoléon, the French general and leader whom Beethoven initially admired. Some people actually compared Napoléon and Beethoven, calling them both revolutionists. There was some truth to that, as even with all of Beethoven's catering to his wealthy patrons, he never lost sight of the effect his works would have on the common people, whom he wanted to enlighten and empower. His view of the French leader changed in 1804 when he heard that Napoléon had declared himself emperor. He scratched out Napoléon's name, which he had written on the title sheet for his new symphony, instead calling it "Sinfonia Eroica, Composed to Celebrate the Memory of a Great Man." Beethoven probably was referring to the man Napoléon was before the French leader let his power go to his head. On the other hand, he may have simply meant it to be a generic title, referring to any heroic individual.

The lengthy work does evoke power and majesty of epic proportions. Audiences were left breathless upon hearing it. In 1809, when Beethoven conducted a repeat performance of the symphony at Vienna for a charity event, Napoléon may have been in the Austrian city. By this time, France was at war with Austria, and Napoléon's soldiers occupied Vienna. It is unclear if Napoléon even knew of his former connection to the symphony, but he did not go to the concert. Napoléon's army won a temporary

## The Best Concert Ever?

The Theater-an-der-Wien, or "theater on the banks of the Wien," in Vienna, was the site of what many critics believe was one of the most important concerts ever. Held just before Christmas, on December 22, 1808, the concert featured a number of Beethoven's works that were played in public for the first time. The program was as follows: Symphony no. 6, a concerto aria called "Ah, perfido," two movements from the Mass in C Major, Beethoven's Fourth Piano Concerto, the Symphony no. 5, and the Choral Fantasy. These works have been performed thousands, perhaps tens of thousands, of times since at concert halls around the world. But on that night, the audience heard the works for the very first time. The concert lasted four hours and was held in an unheated theater. Considering how cold it gets in Vienna during the winter, the length of the concert was a testament to how much people loved Beethoven.

victory in Vienna, but Beethoven's music had already captured the hearts and interest of the public there.

The composer continued to produce other timeless pieces in the following months and years, including his Fourth to Eighth Symphonies; Piano Concerto no. 4, op. 58; Piano Concerto no. 5, op. 73; Emperor, Violin Concerto op. 61; and *Fidelio*, Beethoven's only opera.

## Symphony no. 5, Opus 67

You may not recognize this symphony by its title, but even if you have not listened to much classical music, you probably have heard this piece. It is built around a four-note motif that follows a "dut dut dut daaaah" pattern.

That is oversimplifying its construction, though, because Beethoven took these four notes and built them into what could be the world's most famous symphonic work.

## Symphony no. 6, Opus 68, Pastoral

As the word "pastoral" suggests, this work attempts to re-create the experience of going into a woodland setting. Beethoven composed it while staying at Heiligenstadt, the same place where he wrote his famed testament in 1802.

Even in the nineteenth century, cities were crowded, noisy, and polluted. Many people, not just Beethoven, desired to escape the city to get some fresh air in a more natural setting. Listening to the Pastoral Symphony today, one can imagine how Beethoven felt when he went on one of his woodland retreats.

The symphony is divided into five movements, with titles suggestive of the themes and feelings that the composer hoped to communicate. The first movement is called "Awakening of Cheerful Feelings on Arriving in the Country." The second is "Scene by the Brook," which is followed by "Merry Gathering of the Country Folk," and "Thunderstorm." It concludes with "Shepherd's Song— Happy, Thankful Feelings after the Storm." Clearly, Beethoven associated his rural retreats with joyful times, which he shared with his listeners.

## Symphony no. 7, Opus 92

Beethoven conducted the premiere of this symphony in 1813. The performance was a charitable benefit to help Austrian and Bavarian soldiers who had been wounded during battles against Napoléon's forces. It is a beautiful, uplifting piece that must have reinvigorated war-weary soldiers and their families. Several sources quote Richard Wagner (1813–1883), a famous German composer who was born in the year this symphony debuted, as saying that "if anyone plays the Seventh, tables and benches, cans and cups, the grandmother, the blind and the lame, aye, the children in the cradle fall to dancing." In public on at least one occasion, the otherwise stern and serious Wagner did indeed dance a jig while the Seventh Symphony played!

## Symphony no. 8, Opus 93

Beethoven composed this work in 1812. He often worked on many compositions at the same time. Reflective of his complexity as a person, his pieces were often very dark and gloomy, or extremely upbeat and jolly. Somehow he was able to create such moods in his mind and maintain them at the same time. The Eighth Symphony debuted in public in 1814. It is a lighthearted piece that contrasts with the more pounding and powerful Fifth Symphony and the tranquil moods in the Pastoral Symphony.

# THE CONCERTOS

## Piano Concerto no. 4, Opus 58

During Beethoven's productive Second Period, he did not work on only symphonies. He also composed other works, such as this solo piece for a pianist. It is interesting to note that Beethoven was such an accomplished composer

Beethoven is often depicted as fiery and somewhat crazed in many paintings. In this nineteenth-century etching, however, he is seen in a more relaxed, romantic light.

and musician that few people, even famous and talented musicians, could attempt some of his pieces. After he completed this work in 1806, Beethoven tried to find a pianist who could premiere it. One told him that Piano Concerto no. 4, op. 58 was simply too hard to tackle in a short period. Yet another pianist said he would play it, but then had to substitute another work at the last minute, probably because he could not handle the difficult parts either. Still other pianists tried to play the piece without success. Beethoven himself wound up playing it at a private concert in 1807 to great acclaim.

## Piano Concerto no. 5, Opus 73, Emperor

Beethoven fortunately found a talented pianist—aside from himself—who could play this piece. In February 1812, a student of his, Carl Czerny, debuted the concerto at a Viennese concert. Czerny later became famous for his own piano compositions, but on that night in Vienna, his star shined with Beethoven's.

The Emperor name was not part of the piece's official title, and it is most certain that Beethoven would have never suggested it, given his dislike of Napoléon once the French leader gave himself the title emperor. Instead, some claim that a friend of Beethoven's, Johann Baptist Cramer (1771–1858), once called the concerto the Emperor because of the work's passionate strength. The name has stuck ever since.

## Violin Concerto, Opus 61

In addition to his solo compositions for pianists, Beethoven wrote some memorable works to be played on the violin. This piece is somewhat unusual in that Beethoven had to write it for a specific event, a concert that famous violinist Franz Clement (1780–1842) had arranged. Clement basically made himself the featured performer at his own prearranged concert, and he wanted the talented Beethoven to write a special piece for him. Beethoven did not have much time to put the piece together. In fact, the composer finished it only a few hours before the concert was to begin. Clement probably worked with Beethoven during the writing process, but he still must have been quite anxious on that night. The concert, held December 23, 1806, was a great success with the audience, thanks to the fiery concerto and Clement's nimble playing. Music critics, however, gave it mixed reviews.

# THE OPERA

## Fidelio

It seems appropriate that the writing process of Beethoven's only opera, *Fidelio*, spanned the length of his Second Period. It was heard for the first time in Vienna, in 1805, but reviews were mixed. Beethoven revised it several times before revealing the final version in 1814. *Fidelio* means "fidelity," or "faithfulness." The story is about a noble Spaniard who is locked in a murky dungeon prison by an enemy who hopes to disgrace the poor man and starve him to death. Only the imprisoned man's wife, Leonore, believes that he is innocent, and she risks her own life to save him.

The two-act opera gained fame in the late nineteenth century, when opera companies around the world rediscovered and performed it. While it is a solid effort, critics at the time felt—and many critics still feel today—that the music outshines the overall scope of the piece. Perhaps Beethoven felt more comfortable in his role as a composer of instrumental and vocal music, without the burden of following a dramatic text. His works, after all, did have a dreamy quality that was open to interpretation by listeners. This is true even in pieces, such as the Pastoral, where he suggests themes. Nonetheless, the magnificent music, dramatic vocals, and story line of *Fidelio* make it a popular work among opera buffs to this day.

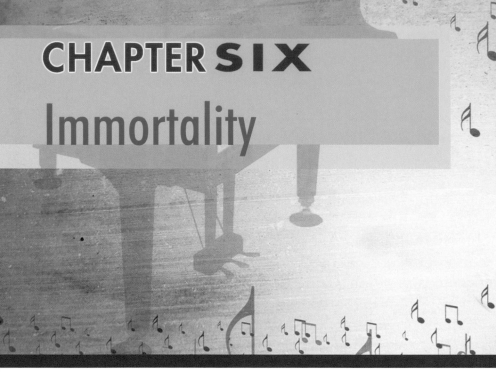

# CHAPTER **SIX**

## Immortality

**W**ork provided Beethoven with an outlet for his creative energies. Unlike many artists who achieved their greatest fame after death (the painter Vincent van Gogh is a good example), Beethoven was famous during his lifetime. Fortunately, he was able to enjoy the money and adulation that came with public recognition. But while his career was an unquestioned success, his personal life was not as easy. His deafness became more profound over time, making it harder for him to communicate with others. He never married and was probably spurned by many women. He also went through an agonizing lawsuit concerning the legal custody of his nephew, an episode that culminated with his nephew attempting suicide.

These thin metal "hearing trumpets" were made especially for Beethoven. Unfortunately, they did not help the composer much when his deafness grew worse.

## DISABILITY WORSENS

Beethoven suffered from many illnesses during his lifetime. For example, his letters reveal that he often experienced abdominal cramps and stomach ailments that made it difficult for him to work. It is not clear what caused these problems, but it could have been a chronic ailment, a virus, or even poison. In the twentieth century, his hair was tested and was found to contain arsenic, a known toxin. The arsenic might have been in the wine he was drinking. It is doubtful that anyone tried to poison the great composer, but the arsenic present in his hair remains a mystery.

What is clear is that Beethoven's deafness worsened as he got older, to the point where he could not carry on a spoken conversation. Instead he carried around notebooks. Friends, family, and colleagues would write something to him in one of the books, and Beethoven would write back a response. This must have been frustrating for Beethoven, who had always found it difficult to communicate through writing.

Beethoven's deafness seemed to heighten his eccentricities. People used to see him walking through the streets of Vienna waving his arms around and mumbling to himself. Hearing aids then were giant amplification tubes, cumbersome devices that looked like tin funnels. Sign language was not yet common. Despite the consoling words of his doctors, Beethoven, for the most part, had to cope with his deafness on his own.

## THE IMMORTAL BELOVED

Beethoven never married, although he probably proposed to at least one woman, Therese von Malfatti, who was the niece of a successful physician friend of Beethoven's. He also enjoyed close relationships with other women, many of whom were the wives of his patrons. There seems to have been a pattern in Beethoven's life, as he often fell in love with unattainable women. They were either married or in a social class that would not accept someone like Beethoven, who was not born into nobility. Of course, some of the women simply were not romantically interested in him.

The composer did have at least one great love affair in his life. The mystery surrounding it is almost as epic and passionate as one of his symphonies. The affair was not revealed during Beethoven's lifetime, but an unsent letter, now known as the "Immortal Beloved," was found

Most experts now believe that Beethoven's "immortal beloved" was Antonie Brentano (right). Unfortunately for the composer, she was already married to his friend, Franz Brentano.

with his belongings. Maynard Solomon reproduces the letter in his book, describing how Beethoven dramatically expressed his love for his "immortal beloved." One section of the letter reads,

> *Good morning, on July 7   Though still in bed, my thoughts go out to you, my Immortal Beloved, not and then joyfully, then sadly, waiting to learn whether or not fate will hear us — I can live only wholly with you or not at all — Yes, I am resolved to wander so long away from you until I can fly to your arms and say that I am really at home with you, and can send my soul enwrapped in you into the lands of spirits — Yes unhappily it must be so — You will be the more contained since you know my fidelity to you. No one else can ever possess my heart — never — never . . .*

*Be calm — love me — today — yesterday — what tearful longings for you — you — you — my life — my all — farewell. Oh continue to love me — never misjudge the most faithful heart of your beloved.*

Beethoven then signed the letter "ever thine," "ever mine," "ever ours."

Beethoven experts now debate the identity of the "immortal beloved." The leading contender seems to be Antonie Brentano, the wife of Beethoven's friend, Franz Brentano. The Brentano family was well connected and helped Beethoven to meet his favorite writer, the German Johann von Goethe. The love letter might have been concealed to protect everyone who was involved, including Beethoven himself.

## KARL BEETHOVEN

Yet another mystery in Beethoven's life concerns his nephew, Karl. In November 1815, Beethoven's brother, Kaspar Carl, died of consumption. He left behind his wife, whom Beethoven detested, and his young son, Karl. When he knew that he was nearing death, Kaspar Carl asked Beethoven to jointly care for Karl with his wife, Johanna. Upon his death, however, Beethoven refused to have anything to do with Johanna. In January 1816, Beethoven sued to gain sole guardianship over Karl. He won.

It is unclear why Karl became such an obsession for Beethoven. Most historians think that because Beethoven did not have a son and heir of his own, he desperately wanted Karl as his adopted son. Beethoven did appear to genuinely care for Karl, whom he would call "dear Karl" and a "sweet" boy in letters.

Karl, however, felt torn between his mother and Beethoven. On at least one occasion, Karl fled Beethoven's home to return to Johanna. Beethoven at first put Karl in a boarding school, but then brought Karl back to his home to be privately tutored. Johanna, during this time, continued to fight to regain custody of her son. Karl, who must have felt emotionally exhausted by the ordeal, tried to commit suicide. Fortunately, the attempt was not successful.

Beethoven received some public humiliation during the court hearings, as it was revealed that his last name really was "van Beethoven," instead of the more aristocratic "von Beethoven." This time Beethoven lost the fight, and the case was closed on July 24, 1820. Beethoven was left heartbroken, humiliated, and without an heir. But music again gave him solace.

## THIRD PERIOD MUSIC

Beethoven's third and final period, which lasted from about 1816 until his death in 1827, included many significant works. Two of the most famous are *Missa solemnis*, or Solemn Mass, and what was to become Beethoven's final symphony, his Symphony no. 9, op. 125. For *Missa solemnis*, Beethoven studied religious compositions written as far back as the sixteenth century. Today's musicians have a lot of written and recorded material to study, but documented music was still in its relative infancy during Beethoven's lifetime. Rare, usually handwritten pieces could be difficult to obtain, but Beethoven persevered. Since he chose a religious theme for this later work, it is possible that he, too, was thinking more about spirituality and his own mortality.

## SYMPHONY NO. 9, OPUS 125

Although Beethoven could have given in to his despair, he worked hard to remain optimistic. These hopeful feelings come through in the famous "Ode to Joy" chorus that he wrote for his ninth, and final, symphony. The words come from the German poet Friedrich Schiller (1759–1805), but they must have resonated with Beethoven. The work concludes,

> *"Be embraced, Millions! Take this kiss for all the world! Brothers, surely a loving Father dwells above the canopy of stars. Do you sink before him, Millions? World, do you sense your Creator? Seek him then beyond the stars! He must dwell beyond the stars."*

It was as though Beethoven himself was pleading with his audience to have faith in others, in all creation, and in God. A stirring, powerful melody adds to the emotional energy of the piece. It is no wonder that the chorus is now a popular work for important celebrations.

## BEETHOVEN'S DEATH AND LEGACY

Beethoven was working on a tenth symphony when his health deteriorated, preventing him from finishing it. In December 1826, he brought Karl home with him to Vienna for a visit. During the trip, Beethoven contracted pneumonia, which worsened his abdominal condition and led to a dangerous buildup of fluids. He also was suffering from liver disease. The combination of illnesses finally led to his death at the age of fifty-six, on March 26, 1827. However, Beethoven did not die without a final display of strength. As biographer Stephen Johnson recounted, several people were with him when he died. One observer, the composer Anselm Huttenbrenner (1794–1868), described what happened:

> *After 5 o'clock there was suddenly a terrific clap of thunder accompanied by a flash of lightning which filled the death-chamber with a harsh light . . . After this unexpected natural occurrence, which shook me greatly, Beethoven opened his eyes, lifted his right hand and looked up for several seconds with his fist clenched and a very serious, threatening expression . . . As he let his hand sink again to the bed, his eyes half closed. My right hand supported his head, my left hand rested on his breast. No more breath, no more heartbeat.*

At some point in your own life, the work of an artist like Beethoven probably affected or influenced you in some way. Perhaps it was a painting, a song, a poem, a movie, a book, or some other form of art that touched you personally and resonated with your own feelings. That is the mark of a great artist. He or she can transcend the apparent limitations of time and space to communicate with others.

Beethoven poured his heart and soul into his works. It is no wonder that his Ninth Symphony was played for an audience of millions in 1989, when the Berlin Wall fell and united Germany. In many of his works, Beethoven expressed love, joy, empowerment, and hope for the future. He understood the timeless nature of these emotions when he referred to his "immortal beloved." Those words now reflect back on Beethoven himself. Through his music, he, too, became immortal and beloved.

# TIMELINE

| | |
|---|---|
| **1770** | Ludwig van Beethoven is baptized in Bonn, on December 17. |
| **1778** | First public recital, on March 26. |
| **1780–1800** | Beethoven's First Period. |
| **1781** | About this time, musician Christian Gottlob Neefe takes on Beethoven as a pupil. |
| **1783** | Neefe puts an announcement in a German music magazine that mentions Beethoven's name and requests funds to send Beethoven to Vienna, Austria. |
| **1787** | Travels to Vienna to visit Mozart; returns to be with his mother, who dies that same year. |
| **1789–1799** | The French Revolution. |
| **1792** | Leaves Bonn for Vienna. His father, Johann, dies. |
| **1793** | Studies with Joseph Haydn. |
| **1796** | Deafness symptoms begin to surface. |
| **1799** | Composes his first symphony, Symphony no. 1 in C Major, op. 21. |
| **1800–1815** | Beethoven's Second Period. |
| **1802** | Writes the Heiligenstadt Testament. |
| **1815–1827** | Beethoven's Third Period. |
| **1816** | Sues to gain guardianship of his nephew, Karl, after the death of his brother. |
| **1820** | Loses the legal case to maintain his guardianship of his nephew. |
| **1826–1827** | Travels with his nephew, Karl, to Vienna and develops pneumonia. |
| **1827** | Dies, on March 26. |

# LIST OF
# SELECTED WORKS

Piano Sonata no. 21 in C Major, op. 53 ("Waldstein") (1804)
Symphony no. 3 in E-flat Major, op. 55 ("Eroica") (1805)
Piano Sonata no. 23 in F Minor, op. 57 ("Appassionata")
    (1804–05)
Symphony no. 5 in C Minor, op. 67 (1808)
Symphony no. 6 in F Major, op. 68 ("Pastorale") (1808)
Piano Concerto no. 5 in E-flat Major, op. 73 ("Emperor")
    (1809–10)
Symphony no. 7 in A Major, op. 92 (1813)
*Fidelio*, op. 72 (1814)
Mass in D Major, op. 123 ("Missa solemnis") (1818–23)
Piano Sonata no. 29 in B-flat Major, op. 106
    ("Hammerklavier") (1819)
Symphony no. 9 in D Minor, op. 125 (1824)
String Quartet in A Minor, op. 132 (1825)
String Quartet in C-sharp Minor, op. 131 (1826)

(Years in parentheses indicate either the time of the
work's composition or the date of its premiere.)

# GLOSSARY

**allegro**  A piece of music that is played at a relatively fast tempo.

**bourgeoisie**  French word that refers to traders, merchants, and other working-class people who represent the class between serfs, or peasants, and the nobility.

**chamber music**  Music for small groups of musicians, with one musician assigned to each part.

**choral music**  Music for choruses, groups of vocalists who sing in unison and usually are organized by the range of their voices.

**classical music**  Music such as symphonies and operas.

**Classicism**  A philosophy for art and life in general that emphasizes order, balance, simplicity, and lack of emotional extremes.

**clavier**  A general term referring to instruments with a keyboard, such as a piano or harpsichord.

**cloister**  A restricted area within a monastery or convent.

**concerto**  A structured musical piece for one or more soloists.

**Enlightenment**  A period in European history when scholars emphasized reason.

**French Revolution**  A war fought between 1789 to 1799. It toppled the French monarchy and resulted in a more democratic form of leadership.

**harpsichord**  An early keyboard instrument.

**key** In musical terms, a system of tones and harmonies that often unifies a composition.

**minuet** A musical composition or movement with a slow, graceful rhythm.

**motif** A short melody, or theme, repeated throughout a longer composition.

**movement** A section or part of a symphony.

**oboe** An instrument with a cylindrical wooden body that is played by blowing into a double reed.

**opera** A work that brings together songs, or solo music, with choral music and instrumentals.

**opus** The Latin word for "work"; often used in the titles of music compositions.

**oratorios** Works that combine solo pieces, chorus work, and instrumentals. Unlike operas, oratorios usually are organized around a general theme, as opposed to a structured drama.

**orchestral music** Works for larger chamber groups and orchestras containing eighty or more musicians.

**patron** One who supports an artist, writer, or cultural institution, such as a museum or opera company.

**Romanticism** A philosophical movement that emphasizes passion, creativity, expressiveness, imagination, and spontaneity.

**scherzo** A quick, lively musical composition or movement.

**symphony** A multi-movement composition played by a group of musicians; it usually consists of four movements, or sections.

**tinnitus** An uncomfortable and distracting ringing in the ears.

# FOR MORE
# INFORMATION

The Beethoven Journal
c/o The American Beethoven Society
Beethoven Center
San Jose State University
One Washington Square
San Jose, CA  95192-0171
(408) 808-2058

Beethoven House Museum
Beethoven-Haus
Bonngasse 18-26
D-53111 Bonn
Germany
+49-228-98175-0

## WEB SITES

Due to the changing nature of Internet links, Rosen
Publishing has developed an online list of Web sites
related to the subject of this book. This site is updated
regularly. Please use this link to access the list:

http://www.rosenlinks.com/mth/bewo

# FOR FURTHER READING

Brasch, Nicolas. *Classical Music and Opera*. Collingwood, ON, Canada: Smart Apple Media, 2004.

Celenza, Anna Harwell. *Farewell Symphony*. Watertown, MA: Charlesbridge Publishing, 2005.

Cencetti, Greta. *Beethoven*. Grand Rapids, MI: School Specialty Children's Publishing, 2001.

Costanza, Stephen. *Mozart Finds a Melody*. New York, NY: Henry Holt Books for Smart Readers, 2004.

January, Brendan. *Ludwig van Beethoven: Musical Genius*. New York, NY: Scholastic Library Publishing, 2004.

Kallan, Stuart A. *History of Classical Music*. Farmington Hills, MI: Lucent Books, 2002.

Livo, Norma. *Troubadour's Storybag: Musical Folktales of the World*. Golden, CO: 1996.

Lynch, Wendy. *Beethoven*. Chicago, IL: Heinemann Library, 2000.

Venezia, Mike. *Ludwig van Beethoven* (Getting to Know the World's Greatest Composers). New York, NY: Scholastic Library Publishing, 1996.

Vernon, Roland. *Beethoven: Introducing*. New York, NY: Chelsea House Publishers, 2000.

# BIBLIOGRAPHY

Balcavage, Denise. *Ludwig van Beethoven: Composer* (Great Achievers, Lives of the Physically Challenged). Philadelphia, PA: Chelsea House Publishers, 1997.

Cooper, Barry. *Beethoven* (The Master Musicians). Oxford, England: Oxford University Press, 2000.

The Classical Music Pages. Retrieved August 2005 (http://w3.rz-berlin.mpg.de/cmp/classmus.html).

Johnson, Stephen. *Ludwig van Beethoven: An Essential Guide to His Life and Works*. London, England: Pavilion Books Limited, 1997.

Pauly, Reinhard. *Music in the Classic Period*. Englewood Cliffs, NJ: Prentice-Hall, 1965.

Schonberg, Harold. *The Lives of the Great Composers*. New York, NY: W. W. Norton & Company Inc., 1970.

Solomon, Maynard. *Beethoven*. New York, NY: Schirmer Trade Books, 1998.

Wade-Matthews, Max, and Wendy Thompson. *The Encyclopedia of Music: Instruments of the Orchestra and the Great Composers*. London, England: Hermes House, 2002.

# INDEX

## ABOUT THE AUTHOR

Jennifer Viegas is a reporter for the Discovery Channel, where she has covered news concerning important historical figures in music, including Beethoven and Mozart. In 2000, she broke the international story about an analysis of a lock of Beethoven's hair. Viegas also serves as a news reporter for Animal Planet, TLC: The Learning Channel, and the Australian Broadcasting Corporation, and she has written books for the Princeton Review and Random House. The author has been listed in Randall's "Who's Who in Music" and plays the French horn, guitar, and several woodwind instruments.

## PHOTO CREDITS

Cover, pp. 11, 19, 45, 49, 51 Beethoven-Haus Bonn; pp. 4, 29 Beethoven-Haus Bonn, Collection H. C. Bodmer; p. 25 © Imagno/ Getty Images; p. 39 © Lebrecht/The Image Works.

**Designer:** Nelson Sá; **Editor:** Christopher Roberts
**Photo Researcher:** Amy Feinberg